The
MIGHTY
JACOB

Israel's Epic Journey

ISBN: 978-0-578-01530-9

Cover Illustration & Design
by Angela Mingeldorff

Printed in the United States of America

A gift to

_____

From

_____

James 1:17 King James Version
Every good gift and every perfect gift is from
above, and cometh down from the Father of
lights, with whom is no variableness, neither
shadow of turning.

The MIGHTY JACOB

Israel's Epic Journey

Written by
BRYAN & MARY BATTLE

Dedication

This book is dedicated to our son, Bryan James Battle, Jr.
You are a wonderful joy to your parents.

Acknowledgements

First, we must thank our heavenly Father who has provided us with His wisdom to share with others. Without Jesus Christ, our Lord and Master, none of our literary endeavors would be possible.

We thank our readers for supporting us in our poetic endeavors as we write God's message. A special recognition goes to Dr. Padmore Enyonam Agbemabiese for his never-ending support and literary encouragement. This book would not be possible without the assistance of his instructive insight. We are also grateful to Ms. Lovie Debnam for her literary assistance.

Sincere appreciation goes out to all our family, friends, and associates who have supported our written works. To the women of Alpha Kappa Alpha Sorority, Incorporated, thank you a million times over. To the brothers of Iota Phi Theta, Fraternity, Incorporated, your brotherly love is unparalleled.

Special Thanks from Mary
I would like to thank my mother, Mary Mines, for bringing me into this world and teaching me God's word at such an early age. A special recognition goes out to my two sisters Beverly and Cordie for your continued support and sisterly love. It means more to me than you will ever know. To my brother Green, thank you for your encouraging critique of our works. A final thank you to my mentor in Christ, Mrs. Peggy Nielsen. I appreciate your time, your prayers, and your insightful thoughts of wisdom. There are so many people that we would like to thank, but it would be impossible to list every name. We are thankful to you all.

The Mighty Jacob is our final poetic endeavor by the Battle family and we are extremely grateful for all who have assisted us in our efforts to spread our written works. Our hope is that you will continue to be enlightened by these written works of art for many years to come.

Genesis 32:24-30 NIV

24 So Jacob was left alone, and a man wrestled with him till daybreak. 25 When the man saw that he could not overpower him, he touched the socket of Jacob's hip so that his hip was wrenched as he wrestled with the man. 26 Then the man said, "Let me go, for it is daybreak." But Jacob replied,
"I will not let you go unless you bless me."
27 The man asked him, "What is your name?"
"Jacob," he answered. 28 Then the man said, "Your name will no longer be Jacob, but Israel, because you have struggled with God and with men and have overcome." 29 Jacob said, "Please tell me your name."
But he replied, "Why do you ask my name?" Then he blessed him there. 30 So Jacob called the place Peniel, saying,
"It is because I saw God face to face, and yet my life was spared."

Introduction

The Mighty Jacob, by Bryan and Mary Battle is a brilliantly insightful book that combines poetry and spirituality in an innovative way that it succeeds elegantly as a beloved inspirational companion for every living soul. In diverse ways, Bryan and Mary Battle teach us to approach the reading of the poems as a spiritual practice, a journey with Jacob, and moreover, as acts of prayer and meditation.

One astonishing thing is that each poem in every chapter of *The Mighty Jacob* is a liberating piece from a solitary contemplative practice to the celebration of the sacred. One needs not be reminded of the story of Jacob when one night he wrestled alone with someone in the dark. Jacob knew that his opponent was stronger and had special powers. In the encounter Jacob declared, "I will not let you go unless you bless me." In similar manner, *The Mighty Jacob* reminds us that, hard as life may seem, our greatest agony, the difficult the challenges we encounter daily, or the most horrible trials on our way may be one of God's way of bringing us His own blessing.

Bryan and Mary Battle are the authors of four previous collections of published poetry—*A Lifetime of Treasures, The Band, Perfumed Legacy, and Fred Frog & Family.* Their spiritual perspectives on Christian life shine through these varied works and are a connoisseur of wonder, because of their attentiveness to moments of trials and the bounties of blessings that lie within them.

Dr. Padmore Agbemabiese is a Professor of English, African-American and African Studies lecturing in the United States. He is a published poet and a playwright. Dr. Agbemabiese is author of the book, *The Smell of Exile* and he has recently written a play titled, *The Journey: From Shackles of Oppression to Mantels of Hope.*

Table of Contents

Chapter One: Heir of Abraham

Chapter Two: Vow

Chapter Three: A Testimony in Jacob

Chapter Four: The Good News

Chapter Five: Israel

CHAPTER 1

HEIR OF

ABRAHAM

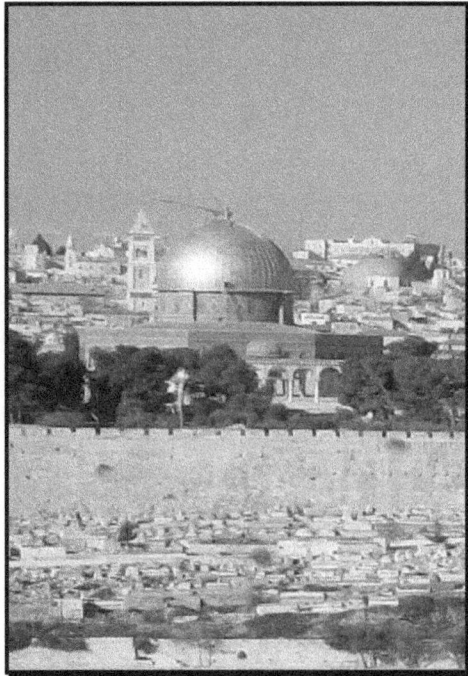

Heir of Abraham

The heir of Abraham is stepping in.
He is claiming his next of kin.

Abraham's descendants are many,
Jacob, Sarah's offspring, and even cousin Benny.

Some heirs have claimed their throne.
It is a righteous one.
It is all God's own.

The heir of Abraham is stepping in.
Many now claim their next of kin.

China, Africa, and the new nation,
of which many are amazingly Asian.

The heir of Abraham is stepping in.
With Jesus Christ, he is claiming his next of kin.

One third of the remnants remain.
This world has gone foolishly insane.

The brothers still fight on the temple mound.
Many are dying on Holy ground.

The heir of Abraham is stepping in.
He is claiming his rightful win.

The heir of Abraham has stepped in.
He is claiming Jesus Christ, his next of kin.

My Father Prayed For Me

My father prayed for me.
My mother, barren after so many years,
She was filled with fear
As we wrestled within her womb.

Two nations were within her.
I grew to become mighty in the Lord.
Yes, it is true, I held Esau's heel
As if it were my sword.

Genesis 25:26 NIV
After this, his brother came out, with his hand grasping Esau's
heel; so he was named Jacob. Isaac was sixty years old when
Rebekah gave birth to them.

Soul's Sanctuary

My soul's sanctuary is oftentimes fervent.
The sanctuary stimulates the soul.
It is a steadfast soul that never grows old.

My soul is a sanctuary of sacred truths.
It does not belong to Abraham, Isaac, or Ruth.

My soul has grown old.
Still, it is a sanctuary of gold.

My soul sanctuary is all my own.
My soul's sanctuary,
It is all that I own.

I was once a child,
Now I am grown.
My soul is no longer my own.

The complexities of a man's worth
Lay in his soul, not in his birth.

Genesis 25:33
But Jacob said, "Swear to me first." So he swore an oath to him,
selling his birthright to Jacob.

Mother, Father

My mother desires that I be the blessed son of Isaac.
My father, old and weary, he cannot see.
Does he even know that he just blessed me?

Oh Mother, Father, what is Esau going to do to me?

It was Rebekah who is to blame.
I was just obeying my mother's name.

Father, bless me this day.
Mother, God forgives you.
Let us pray.

Genesis 27:8-10
8 Now, my son, listen carefully and do what I tell you: 9 Go out to the flock and bring me two choice young goats, so I can prepare some tasty food for your father, just the way he likes it. 10 Then take it to your father to eat, so that he may give you his blessing before he dies."

Between Judgment and Mercy

Between judgment and mercy, there is a biblical devise.
Between judgment and mercy, the darkness cries.

Judgment comes from God above.
Mercy flows in like an olive leaf
Being carried by the dove.

Rebekah deceitfully yearns.
God's mercy, she has not earned.

He gave it freely.
Salvation comes only through one seed.
Between judgment and mercy, God blesses me.

Genesis 27:14-16 NIV
14 So he went and got them and brought them to his mother, and
she prepared some tasty food, just the way his father liked it. 15
Then Rebekah took the best clothes of Esau her older son, which
she had in the house, and put them on her younger son Jacob. 16
She also covered his hands and the smooth part of his neck with
the goatskins.

Kiss Me My Son

Come near to me.
Kiss me, my son.
I have given you the blessing
That cannot be undone.

The Lord has blessed you richly.
Nations will bow down to you
In glorious reverence to our God.

Genesis 27:26 NIV
26 Then his father Isaac said to him,
"Come here, my son, and kiss me."

The Path

The path we journey is not our own.
God reigns eternally on His throne.
One day, we shall all go to our glorious home.

The path to prosperity is a healthy view
Of the old and the new.

This path never ends.
It is everlasting, my friend!

Genesis 27:28-29 NIV
28 May God give you of heaven's dew
and of earth's richness—
an abundance of grain and new wine.

29 May nations serve you
and peoples bow down to you.
Be lord over your brothers,
and may the sons of your mother bow down to you.
May those who curse you be cursed
and those who bless you be blessed."

Never Know

We shall never know the entire mystery of God.
The greatness of His power,
It appears to many people as odd.

We shall never know.
One shall reap.
The other shall sow.

We shall never know our God given destiny
Until we ask the Lord to take complete control.
This, my friend, we shall never know.

Genesis 27:39-40
39 His father Isaac answered him,
"Your dwelling will be
away from the earth's richness,
away from the dew of heaven above.

40 You will live by the sword
and you will serve your brother.
But when you grow restless,
you will throw his yoke
from off your neck."

Flee At Once

Flee at once, my son.
Flee from here.
Your brother is engulfed with anger.
He has no fear.

Flee at once, my son.
Esau desires to kill you.
Flee at once from this place,
And go to Laban.

My son, may the Almighty God of our fathers bless
You this day.
Flee at once.
This I do pray.

Genesis 27:41-43 NIV
42 When Rebekah was told what her older son Esau had said, she sent for her younger son Jacob and said to him, "Your brother Esau is consoling himself with the thought of killing you. 43 Now then, my son, do what I say: Flee at once to my brother Laban in Haran

The Ladder

I look to the ladder
And I see angels ascending on earth.

I look to the ladder, as I dream.
The angels are descending from Thee.

To You, my Lord, I see the dream
You have given only to me.

Keep me oh Lord.
Surely, You will feed me.
The tenth, I shall give unto Thee.

Genesis 28:12 NIV
12 He had a dream in which he saw a stairway resting on the earth, with its top reaching to heaven, and the angels of God were ascending and descending on it.

My Friend

My Friend controls the mighty men.
He has control from within.

My Friend controls the horses.
He even causes the river to flow upstream.
He controls the happy and the mean.

My Friend is the Prophet of old.
He is the God of humankind's silver and gold.

My Friend is the Rose of Sharon.
He gives hope to the motherless.
He gives comfort to the barren.

My Friend gives me peace,
So that I may forever breathe.

My Friend gives me vision.
He sets me forth on His mission.

My Friend loves me.
It is in God alone that I live, move, and breathe.

I Shall Meet

I shall meet my brother today.
Before I journey, to the Lord I must pray.

Divide my company into two bands.
I am not sure if he will have mercy on this man.

Oh Lord, my Lord, I know what you say of my seed.
They shall be as the sand of the sea.

I shall meet my brother today.
Heavenly Father, guide my family along the way.

Genesis 33:1 (New International Version)

[1] *Jacob looked up and there was Esau, coming with his four hundred men; so he divided the children among Leah, Rachel and the two maidservants.*

Arise

Jacob, remember the pillar.
Remember the vow.
Arise, go now.

Get out of the land.
Flee at once from Laban.

Genesis 31:13 NIV
13 I am the God of Bethel, where you anointed a pillar and
where you made a vow to me. Now leave this land
at once and go back to your native land.' "

Bless Me

I will hold on to You.
I will never let go.
I will hold on,
Whether in the heat of the dessert,
Or in the chilling cold.

My hands are lifted high.
Your presence surrounds me.
You encompass my body.

Limping into the morning light,
Having survived through the frightful night.

I hold You close and shall not let go
Unless You bless me.
This I promise You.
This I certainly know.

Bless me my Lord
And then I shall let You go.

Genesis 32:26 NIV
26 Then the man said, "Let me go, for it is daybreak."
But Jacob replied, "I will not let you go unless you bless
me."

The Wounded Soul

The soul does not foresee encounters of life.
It oftentimes becomes wounded, clinging to heartless strife.

Quite often, the soul is painted
With the scent of a hidden past.

This soul, though wounded, grasps for life to see,
Weeping no longer with tears of sorrow,
Jacob knows what is the future of God's tomorrow.

Genesis 49 (New International Version)

Genesis 49
*1 Then Jacob called for his sons and said: "Gather around so I
can tell you what will happen to you in days to come.*

*2 "Assemble and listen, sons of Jacob;
listen to your father Israel.*

*3 "Reuben, you are my firstborn,
my might, the first sign of my strength,
excelling in honor, excelling in power.*

*4 Turbulent as the waters, you will no longer excel,
for you went up onto your father's bed,
onto my couch and defiled it.*

*5 "Simeon and Levi are brothers—
their swords are weapons of violence.*

6 Let me not enter their council,
  let me not join their assembly,
for they have killed men in their anger
and hamstrung oxen as they pleased.

7 Cursed be their anger, so fierce,
  and their fury, so cruel!
I will scatter them in Jacob
and disperse them in Israel.

8 "Judah, your brothers will praise you;
your hand will be on the neck of your enemies;
your father's sons will bow down to you.

9 You are a lion's cub, O Judah;
  you return from the prey, my son.
Like a lion he crouches and lies down,
like a lioness—who dares to rouse him?

10 The scepter will not depart from Judah,
nor the ruler's staff from between his feet,
  until he comes to whom it belongs
and the obedience of the nations is his.

11 He will tether his donkey to a vine,
  his colt to the choicest branch;
he will wash his garments in wine,
  his robes in the blood of grapes.

12 His eyes will be darker than wine,
  his teeth whiter than milk.

13 "Zebulun will live by the seashore
  and become a haven for ships;
his border will extend toward Sidon.

14 "Issachar is a rawboned donkey
lying down between two saddlebags.

15 When he sees how good is his resting place
and how pleasant is his land,
he will bend his shoulder to the burden
and submit to forced labor.

16 "Dan will provide justice for his people
as one of the tribes of Israel.

17 Dan will be a serpent by the roadside,
a viper along the path,
that bites the horse's heels
so that its rider tumbles backward.

18 "I look for your deliverance, O LORD.

19 "Gad will be attacked by a band of raiders,
but he will attack them at their heels.

20 "Asher's food will be rich;
he will provide delicacies fit for a king.

21 "Naphtali is a doe set free
that bears beautiful fawns.

22 "Joseph is a fruitful vine,
a fruitful vine near a spring,
whose branches climb over a wall.

23 With bitterness archers attacked him;
they shot at him with hostility.

24 But his bow remained steady,
his strong arms stayed limber,
because of the hand of the Mighty One of Jacob,
because of the Shepherd, the Rock of Israel,

25 because of your father's God, who helps you,
because of the Almighty, who blesses you
with blessings of the heavens above,
blessings of the deep that lies below,
blessings of the breast and womb.

26 Your father's blessings are greater
than the blessings of the ancient mountains,
than the bounty of the age-old hills.
Let all these rest on the head of Joseph,
on the brow of the prince among his brothers.

27 "Benjamin is a ravenous wolf;
in the morning he devours the prey,
in the evening he divides the plunder."

28 All these are the twelve tribes of Israel, and this is what their
father said to them when he blessed them, giving each the blessing
appropriate to him.

The Touch

The secrets of olden days cry out to the soul.
Jacob, finding himself crippled by the reality of his dream,
Wakes to find his life forever changed.
It was not a dream but that which is reality.
It is what the eye can see.

He touched the hollow of his thigh.
Though wounded by the touch of the Almighty One,
Jacob remained strong, although he desired to cry.

Genesis 32:32 NIV
32 Therefore to this day the Israelites do not eat the tendon
attached to the socket of the hip, because the socket of Jacob's hip
was touched near the tendon.

Order

God creates order from disaster.
God is the perfect Master.

Every step, He must order.
He shall protect us from the enemy's border.

God is a God of order.
Respect travels in conjunction with the Lord's order.
Children of God, move beyond the palace border!

God commands order of His people.
Some are free.
Some are equal.

God chastises His children.
Those who hear Him are free from sin.

Genesis 41:40
You shall be in charge of my palace, and all my people are to submit to your orders. Only with respect to the throne will I be greater than you.

O Jacob

O Jacob, God desires your soul.
Man of God, you are growing old.

O Jacob, weary you may be.
I am not you, and you are not me!

Jacob, you are chasing a dream.
Jacob, your women and children are a bit mean.

O Jacob, your children have plenty.
The Just One of Israel blesses your seed.
He is the Almighty King.

Joseph, Ruler Over Egypt

Joseph, I have honestly loved you more than your brothers.
It is not because of your beloved mother.

You are the son of my olden days.
Because of the Almighty God, we can give Him praise.

You have always been a blessed son of Jacob.
The coat of many colors was given only to you, my son.

Joseph, I have loved you with all my might.
My heart sank, the day I was told by your brothers
You were no longer alive.

My son did not die.
I have seen my beloved Joseph with my own eyes.

My soul rejoices in the sight of you.
Tears stream down my face as I embrace you.

The Lord told me that my seed would be a great nation.
You were chosen by God and are a part of His creation.

Joseph, ruler over all of Egypt.
My son, you have been a joy to your father.
Your brothers, I shall not bother.

Genesis 41:42 NIV
*42 Then Pharaoh took his signet ring from his finger and put it
on Joseph's finger. He dressed him in robes of fine linen and
put a gold chain around his neck.*

Jehovah

Jehovah's Word is everlasting.
His love is an alabaster.

Jehovah's fire is eternally consuming.
His peace passes all human understanding.

Jehovah's fire is the Prophet of old.
This is the story His sons and daughters are told.

Jehovah breathes life from dust.
He brings forth gold from rust.

The Spirit of God is eternally consuming.
Our God is always pruning.

Numbers 23:23 NIV
23 There is no sorcery against Jacob,
no divination against Israel.
It will now be said of Jacob
and of Israel, 'See what God has done!'

CHAPTER 2

VOW

Vow

My Lord, you have come to me
To show me the way in which I must journey.
You have promised to me perpetual blessings
That will continue through my seed.

God, I vow to you this day,
Be with me my Lord.
Protect me along the way.

As I rise up early for my travels,
I pour out holy oil on this pillar.

Keep me.
Feed me.

Allow me to do God's will.
Protect me from evil
So that I may never have to kill.

My vow to You oh Lord, one tenth.
I must return this portion
Of everything before it is spent.

Numbers 24:17 NIV
17 "I see him, but not now;
I behold him, but not near.
A star will come out of Jacob;
a scepter will rise out of Israel.
He will crush the foreheads of Moab,
the skulls of all the sons of Sheth.

Truth

Truth brings forth the vision
As God makes it plain.
It is man who has gone utterly insane.

Truth is on a mission from the Just One of Israel.
This Truth, even Naomi and Ruth could feel.

God's Truth is clear to me.
I cannot see you.
Do you not see the sea?

God is true.
All that He speaks,
He shall do.

Deuteronomy 33:10 NIV
10 He teaches your precepts to Jacob
and your law to Israel.
He offers incense before you
and whole burnt offerings on your altar..

Hidden

Nothing is hidden from God.
He appears unto many as mysteriously odd.

His Truth is not hidden.
It is in the Holy Scriptures.
It is clearly written.

Hidden is His imminent return.
Hidden, He shall never be.
He is our God.
We are forever free.

Hidden in my heart,
Sealed upon my soul.
My love for my Messiah
Shall never wax cold.

Hidden, this light shall forever shine.
Hidden, this vessel belongs to the one Divine.

Deuteronomy 33:19
They will summon peoples to the mountain and there offer
sacrifices of righteousness; they will feast on the abundance of the
seas, on the treasures hidden in the sand."

As Time Passes By

As time passes by,
Much of humanity hides.

No words can express
His hidden blessed.

As time passes by,
The family grows stronger.
As time passes by,
Some continue to live
While others wait a little while longer.

As time passes us by
Many will live,
Some will die.

As time passes by,
Many will gain power.
As time passes by,
The world will see the final hour.

2 Kings 5:15 NIV
15 Then Naaman and all his attendants went back to the man of
God. He stood before him and said, "Now I know that there is
no God in all the world except in Israel. Please accept now a gift
from your servant."

Heart

The heart of God is never odd.
It is a heart held by only One.

The heart is that of God's only begotten Son.
The heart of God forever speaks.
This heart doth not always speak peace.

The heart of God brings a Sword.
This Sword is God's holy Word.

The heart of man
is broken once again.

Just as the heart pumps blood,
God gives us his eternal love.

2 Kings 22:19
Because your heart was responsive and you humbled yourself
before the LORD when you heard what I have spoken against this
place and its people, that they would become accursed and laid
waste, and because you tore your robes and wept in my presence, I
have heard you, declares the LORD.

God's Program

God's program is a written agenda.

God's program allows us to set our goals.
When we cannot reach them,
He reminds us that they are not in His agenda.

God's program is His Word.
His program comes with no special guide.
Only with Christ can one eternally glide.

God's program comes with assistance.
The Holy Spirit flows with no resistance.

Isaiah 57:15
For this is what the high and lofty One says— he who lives forever,
whose name is holy: "I live in a high and holy place, but also with
him who is contrite and lowly in spirit, to revive the spirit of the
lowly and to revive the heart of the contrite.

Trumpet

The trumpet of the Lord sounds the alarm.
The great deceiver is using his spiritual charm.

Watch and pray,
For this is the day.

God is calling His people.
Some are free, while others are equal.

The trumpet of God sounds.
All will hear His word on the mound.

The trumpet of God calls on Israel.
God does hear.
God does feel.

His people hear Him sounding the alarm.
We will be caught up with no harm.

Jeremiah 4:19
Oh, my anguish, my anguish! I writhe in pain. Oh, the agony of my heart! My heart pounds within me, I cannot keep silent. For I have heard the sound of the trumpet; I have heard the battle cry.

Promise

Promise is God's way of restoring His covenant.
God's promise to His people will come.

Restoration is all but won.
Restoration shall come from the Just One of Israel.

These are God's promises for the young and old.
These are the promises his servants are told.

The promise of Abraham stands.
The promise is to God's women, children, and men.

The promise stands with God.
The promise may seem to family as odd.

The promise to Abraham still stands.
It stands clearly on one man.

Ezekiel 11:16
"Therefore say: 'This is what the Sovereign LORD says: Although I sent them far away among the nations and scattered them among the countries, yet for a little while I have been a sanctuary for them in the countries where they have gone.'

Dreamer

Dreamer, tell me what you see.
Dreamer, earth is not falling into the sea.

Dreamer, you see a ladder and the Lord.
Dreamer, tell me some more.

Dreamer, your dreams are strangely real.
Dreamer, it is reality that you feel.

Dreamer, Babylon is no more.
Dreamer, man is attacking with the great boar.

Dreamer, the world is under a spell.
Angels are ascending to Heaven.
Others are descending, while
Hearing the final bell.

Dreamer, I see.
Dreamer, you believe.

Dreamer, the world is a fire rising.
Dreamer, the deceiver is still despising.

Dreamer, they look at you as a mystery.
Jesus Christ is the Prince of Peace.

Job 5:17-18
17 "Blessed is the man whom God corrects;
so do not despise the discipline of the Almighty.

18 For he wounds, but he also binds up;
he injures, but his hands also heal.

CHAPTER 3

A TESTIMONY
IN JACOB

Consecrate

Consecrate yourselves
Before stepping into God's holy temple.

Go in and purify the temple.
Remove all that is unclean.

Consecrate yourselves.
Stop looking so mean.

2 Chronicles 32:33 NIV
33 Hezekiah rested with his fathers and was buried on the hill
where the tombs of David's descendants are. All Judah and the
people of Jerusalem honored him when he died. And Manasseh
his son succeeded him as king.

Wisdom and Fools

Fools despise wisdom
Wisdom is an enemy of ignorance.

Fools carry around lamps with no oil.
Wisdom dwells in the presence of God's spoil.

Wisdom knows the holy Lamb.
Fools look to similarities of man.

Proverbs 14:8 (New International Version)

*[8] The wisdom of the prudent is to give thought to their ways,
but the folly of fools is deception*

Spirit & Truth

From David to Solomon,
From Naomi and Ruth,
One must worship God in Spirit and Truth.

Spirit & Truth lives through Jesus Christ.
Truth comes with no lies.
The Holy Spirit is not in disguise.

The God of Spirit is the God of Truth.
He is the God of Naomi, Jacob, and Ruth.

The Holy Spirit guides God's children.
Those who are in Christ are no longer children of women and men.

Spirit & Truth speaks life
Despite a humanity of momentary strife.

God speaks Truth through His Word.
It is the Spirit of God, which is a double-edged Sword.

Ezra 8:35 NIV
35 Then the exiles who had returned from captivity sacrificed burnt offerings to the God of Israel: twelve bulls for all Israel, ninety-six rams, seventy-seven male lambs and, as a sin offering, twelve male goats. All this was a burnt offering to the LORD.

Mercy

Mercy rushes in.
Mercy covers the men, children, and women.

Mercy sees the chosen people.
Mercy does not rest, nor is it always equal.

Mercy rushes into the Holy land.
Mercy sees the God of man.

Ezra 10:1 NIV
1 While Ezra was praying and confessing, weeping and
throwing himself down before the house of God, a large crowd
of Israelites—men, women and children—gathered around
him. They too wept bitterly.

Tribal Mothers

The tribal mothers are many.
They have much.
They desire plenty.

Rachel weeps for her children.
Benjamin sees the suffering of his next of kin.

Beside the pools of water
Are the mothers who brought her.

Next to the empty tomb
Lay one more son, torn from the womb.

These tribal mothers possess scars of plenty.
We lament under the tree of many.

There is no profit under the sun.
God knows all that is done and undone.

The tribal mother is weeping over her child's grave,
No longer bound, no longer a slave.

Nehemiah 10:33 NIV
33 for the bread set out on the table; for the regular grain
offerings and burnt offerings; for the offerings on the Sabbaths,
New Moon festivals and appointed feasts; for the holy offerings;
for sin offerings to make atonement for Israel; and for all the
duties of the house of our God.

Peculiar Treasure

There is a peculiar treasure of kings.
Many have found it in a kiss.
Some have found it in a ring.

Peculiar are these treasures, looking to gods.
Peculiar are the people, finding Christ's love odd.

Many do not labor in wisdom.
Much find laughter with sorrow.
Peculiar are the treasures of God's tomorrow.

Psalm 14:7 NIV
7 Oh, that salvation for Israel would come out of Zion!
When the LORD restores the fortunes of his people,
let Jacob rejoice and Israel be glad!

CHAPTER 4

THE GOOD NEWS

The Good News

The good news of God
Is never looked upon as odd.
The good news of God
Is His Omnipotent Holy Ghost power.
The good news comes
Even in the final hour.

The good news of God
Is no mystery, not even to the fraud.

The good news is His word.
It is the Holy Sword, which we do gird.

The good news travels from devastation to restoration.
All the promises of God pass from generation to generation.

The good news is worthy of all praise.
Christ shall be worshipped through all of our days.

Proverbs 15:30
A cheerful look brings joy to the heart, and good news gives health
to the bones.

Zion

Zion, it is time.
Jesus is the Messiah,
The only Divine.

Zion, God calls your name.
Israel, God has made it plain.

Rejoice, my beloved Jacob.
Be glad, for salvation has come.

Psalm 2:6
"I have installed my King on Zion, my holy hill."

The God of Jacob

Oh Lord, be a defense for me
Against my enemy.
Hear my cry, oh God of Jacob.

The day of trouble is at hand.
Heavenly Father, help this mighty man.

Hide me in the day of calamity.
Lord, please protect my family.

My God, keep me not away from Your secret place.
Protect me in this last and evil day.
Hear me Lord, as I pray.

Psalm 14:7
Oh, that salvation for Israel would come out of Zion! When the LORD restores the fortunes of his people, let Jacob rejoice and Israel be glad!

Face To Face

I have seen Him face to face.
I lift my hands and give Him praise.

I have seen Elohim.
My God eternally reigns supreme.

Psalm 22:23 NIV
23 You who fear the LORD, praise him!
All you descendants of Jacob, honor him!
Revere him, all you descendants of Israel!

Psalm

Son of David, speak a word.
Son of Abraham, what have you heard?

I sing a psalm
For those going home.

I speak a word that no man has heard.
I seek Your face and gird.

Psalm 24:6
Such is the generation of those who seek him, who seek your face,
O God of Jacob. Selah

Mighty Jacob

Jacob, My son
Jacob, your descendants are not done.

Mighty you are.
Your people shall travel
Near and far.
Some may never know
Who they really are.

Israel, educate your children.
Teach them to love their neighbor
And their next of kin.

Jacob, remember your staff.
Israel, remember to live, love, and laugh.

Psalm 78:5 NIV
5 He decreed statutes for Jacob
and established the law in Israel,
which he commanded our forefathers
to teach their children,

He Is Alive

He is alive.
I know this is true.

He is alive in me.
He is alive in you.

I can feel Him looking down upon me.
I stop, look up, and breathe.

He is in the air I breathe.
He is the only begotten Seed.
From generation to generation,
It is because of Christ that I live, move, and believe!

He is alive and is risen.
Risen, He shall forever remain.
One day, He shall come for us again.

Until that great day of His imminent return,
We shall desire more of Him and steadfast we yearn.

Psalm 78:71 NIV
71 from tending the sheep he brought him
to be the shepherd of his people Jacob,
of Israel his inheritance.

Flowered Finery

Flowered finery need not man to breathe.
Flowered finery springs forth from One mighty seed.

Fine is His kingdom.
Perfect is His drum.
Flowered finery has won.

The flower flourishes.
She is like a lily in the field.

Flowered to perfection are His lilies of the valley.
Pure is His affection, brought forth from the colorful galley.

Psalm 103:15
As for man, his days are like grass, he flourishes like a flower of the field;

Mighty Man

Oh Lord, my Lord, my tribes are spread throughout the land.
Dear Lord, help this mighty man!

Father, I need you to be my guide
As my strength is crippled in my thigh.
Oh Lord, a mighty man, am I?

Psalm 104:33-34
33 I will sing to the LORD all my life;
I will sing praise to my God as long as I live.

34 May my meditation be pleasing to him,
as I rejoice in the LORD.

Treasures of Darkness

My beloved Israel
I have given you the
Treasures of Darkness.

My son, you are not ruined.
You must seek that which is hidden from man.

Search for the hidden Treasures of Darkness.
There, you will find a way out of the world's mess.

Israel, I have brought you forth from
My secret place so that you may know
My Almighty face.

Isaiah 45:3 NIV
3 I will give you the treasures of darkness,
riches stored in secret places,
so that you may know that I am the LORD,
the God of Israel, who summons you by name.

Dispersed

Dispersed, I shall not always be.
God desires more of me.

Dispersed throughout the world,
God has guided and carried the little
Boy and girl.

Israel's seed has been dispersed throughout the world.
God still demands more of the little boy and the little girl.

Twelve tribes travel the world.
God shall rise up in them as a treasured pearl.

Dispersed, they shall not always be.
I shall bring them back and gather them unto Me.

Ezekiel 37:21
and say to them, 'This is what the Sovereign LORD says: I will take the Israelites out of the nations where they have gone. I will gather them from all around and bring them back into their own land.

CHAPTER 5

ISRAEL

O Israel

Hear, O Israel is God's key.
Here Israel, can you see Me?

Hear, O Israel is God's great key.
Here, O Israel, it is Christ that you see.

Hear, O Israel, your Messiah calling your name.
Israel, the world has gone utterly insane.

Isaiah 49:3 (New International Version)

*[3] He said to me, "You are my servant,
Israel, in whom I will display my splendor."*

Our Lord

Our Lord died for all.
Our Lord did rise in the presence of a few.

Our Lord is risen.
Jesus Christ remains King for all of humankind to see.

Our Lord did choose you!
Our Lord did choose me.
Our Lord, who already knew why we remain free!

It is the grace and mercy from the east to the west.
It is God at His very best!

I can see Israel's sons of God and men of valor!
I can see the cry of the daughters of Zion who no longer scatter!

I see the little children surrounding God and sitting on His lap!
I see victory through the Just One of Israel.
I rejoice in the Lord.
I am healed.

Israel, open your eyes.
Beloved, God is no surprise!

Galatians 3:26-29
26You are all sons of God through faith in Christ Jesus, 27for all of you who were baptized into Christ have clothed yourselves with Christ. 28There is neither Jew nor Greek, slave nor free, male nor female, for you are all one in Christ Jesus. 29If you belong to Christ, then you are Abraham's seed, and heirs according to the promise.

The Portion of Jacob

He is the Portion of Jacob.
He is the Maker of all things.
He is King of kings.

He is the Portion of Jacob.
He is God Almighty.

He is the God of Abraham,
No longer Abram.

He is the Portion of Jacob,
Now Israel.
He is even the God of brother Bill.

He is the Portion of Jacob.
He holds hidden Israel's portion.
He brings together His chosen.

Who is He?
He is the Portion of Jacob,
The Maker of all things.

He is the Messiah.
He is King of all kings.

Jeremiah 10:16
He who is the Portion of Jacob is not like these, for he is the Maker of all things, including Israel, the tribe of his inheritance—the LORD Almighty is his name.

Days of Old

From the days of old
My people are told,
The last shall be first.
In Christ do we thirst.

The days of old
Are growing hot, not cold.

The earth is growing weary.
God's truth is flowing clearly.

God speaks the same language in multiple love lines.
From the days of old, His truth never dies.

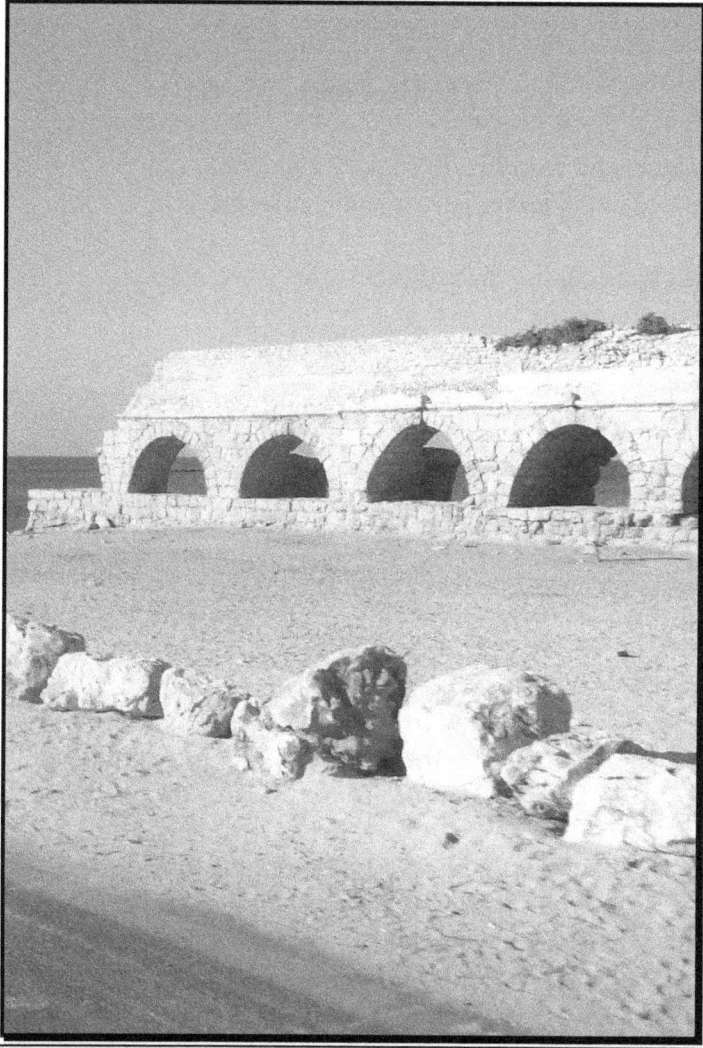

The Face of the World

The face of the world is drastically changing.
Some faces look alike, yet are quite amazing.

God is changing the face of the world.
God is saving the little boy and the little girl.

Redemption shall come
From the Just One.

Israel, it is blooming season.
Oh my servant Jacob, I Am the reason.

Isaiah 27:6 NIV
6 In days to come Jacob will take root,
Israel will bud and blossom
and fill all the world with fruit.

Revelation 21:11-13 (New International Version)
11It shone with the glory of God, and its brilliance was like
that of a very precious jewel, like a jasper, clear as crystal.
12It had a great, high wall with twelve gates, and with
twelve angels at the gates. On the gates were written the
names of the twelve tribes of Israel. 13There were three
gates on the east, three on the north, three on the south and
three on the west.

Machpelah

Promise me you will bury me
In the land of my people.

Bury me with my fathers.
Take me to the cave.

Swear to me that you will carry me home.
Do not leave me in this foreign land.
Bury me as the mighty Jacob.
Lay me to rest as the man I am.

Bury me in Machpelah.
Lay me near my beloved Leah.

Genesis 49:29-31 NIV
29 Then he gave them these instructions: "I am about to be gathered to my people. Bury me with my fathers in the cave in the field of Ephron the Hittite, 30 the cave in the field of Machpelah, near Mamre in Canaan, which Abraham bought as a burial place from Ephron the Hittite, along with the field. 31 There Abraham and his wife Sarah were buried, there Isaac and his wife Rebekah were buried, and there I buried Leah.

ABOUT THE AUTHORS

From the writers of *A Lifetime of Treasures* comes another unique collection of written wisdom. Bryan & Mary's brilliant biblically based works of art are thought provoking, illuminating, and lyrical words of insightful thought.

Bryan James Battle, Sr. was born in Columbus, Ohio, the fifth of six children. He enjoys coaching little league football, movie going, and traveling. He is also a life member of his fraternity; Iota Phi Theta Fraternity, Inc. Bryan is also a member of Phi Beta Kappa Honor Society.

Mary was born in Youngstown, Ohio. She is a graduate of The Ohio State University and Ohio Dominican University. Mary enjoys spending time volunteering with members of her sorority, Alpha Kappa Alpha Sorority, Inc.

They are the proud parents of Bryan James Battle, Jr. Bryan Jr. is a student at Oakland Park Traditional School in Columbus, Ohio. He enjoys playing chess, writing with his parents, and playing football.

ABOUT THE ILLUSTRATOR

Angela Marie Mingledorff was born in Beaufort, South Carolina. Her father, David and mother Barbara Zeoli were born in Philadelphia, Pennsylvania. Her father made the military his career and her mother was a nurse. Angela grew up in a military atmosphere and was always moving. She lived in the state of New Jersey, South Carolina, and Hawaii.

After graduating Beaufort High School in 2000, Angela wanted to find her calling in life. Even from an early age she enjoyed drawing and is now a self-taught artist. She found a passion in capturing peoples expressions through portraits.

Throughout her life she has enjoyed being employed in the dental field and child development but always wanted to pursue her dreams of making a career out of her exquisite art. She has created dozens of family portraits by bringing together many individuals pictures.

Angela is a native of Beaufort, South Carolina. She and her husband, Walter, reside on Lady's Island, South Carolina and are the parents of two young children, Randy and Haley. The lovely couple is expecting their third child, Sarah, in 2009.

View additional works by Angela Marie at
www.artwanted.com/angelamarie

Additional Books by Battle Enterprise

Our publishing goal is to spread the wisdom of one family's journey through life. Our family has taken on the daunting task of discovering our past, writing through the present, and looking into our future through poetic thought. We write down our feelings in the most simplistic form known to man, poetry. We have narrowed our writings down to a compilation of poetry and spoken word through the life of a multi-racial, multi-ethnic, monotheistic family.

As we research and trace our heritage and racial makeup, we learn more about life and how we connect to those we love and cherish.

ISBN: 978-1-4259-8395-6

AVAILABLE AT AUTHORHOUSE, BARNES & NOBLE, AMAZON, AND BOOKSTORES EVERYWHERE

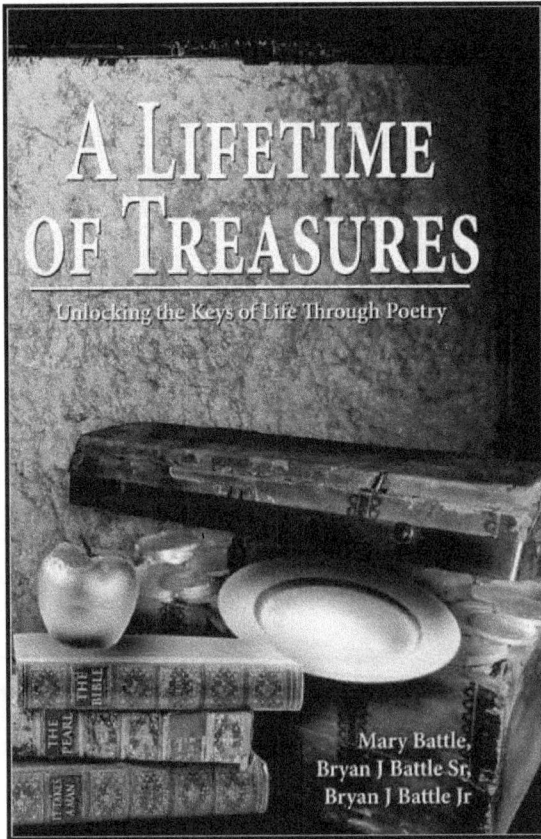

A LIFETIME OF TREASURES
Unlocking the Keys of Life Through Poetry

Mary Battle,
Bryan J Battle Sr,
Bryan J Battle Jr

An innovative and unique poetic voice, Bryan Battle Sr, and Bryan Battle Jr. take the reader on a man's journey back into time, through the hearts of their understanding as they enter the delicate realm of American life. In their writings, The Battle family tackle such issues as the African-American males in prison, the negative stereotypes of African-Americans in America and the Diaspora, and the exploration of financial success through business and land ownership. Journey with us as we build upon our strong foundations in *The Band* of life.

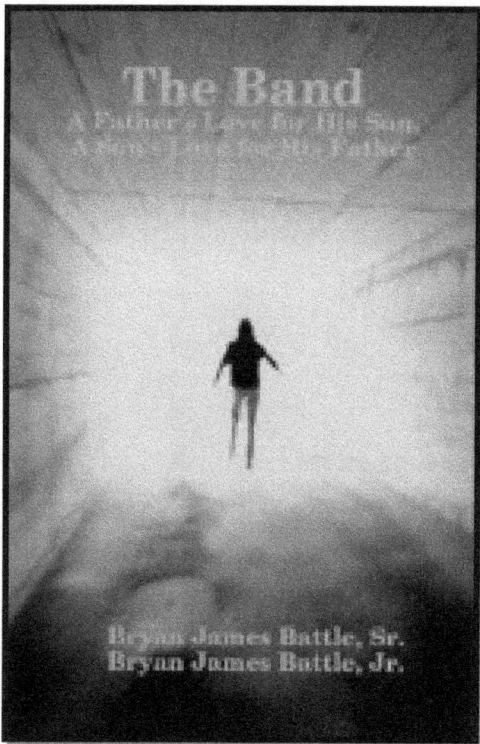

ISBN: 978-1-6058-5592-9

AVAILABLE AT
WWW.LIFETIMEOFTREASURES.COM

Perfumed Legacy is a collection of poetry written by Mary Ann Battle and Beverly Joyce Cosey, two biological sisters and members of Alpha Kappa Alpha Sorority, Inc. Join them as they enter into a journey of sisterhood of poetic thought with no limits. The alabasters of love from these sisters are illuminated on each page.

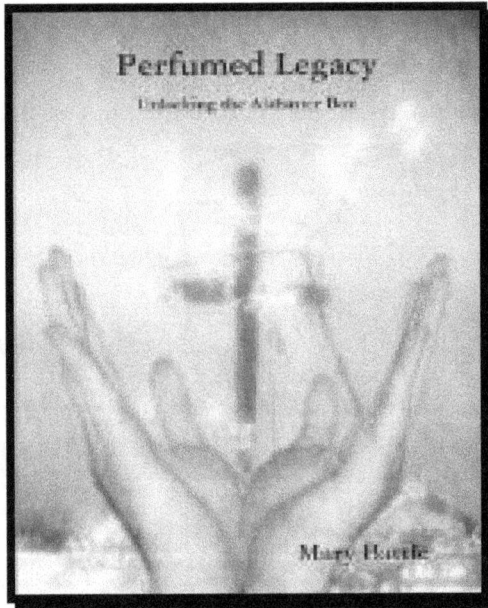

AVAILABLE AT

WWW.LIFETIMEOFTREASURES.COM

INTRODUCING... OUR FIRST BOOK FOR

YOUNG READERS

Meet the newest member of the family, Fred Frog. Fred invites you to his world of family, fun, and education. Join us as we learn how poetry can help a young reader achieve greatness. Reading is achieving. Reading is succeeding!

AVAILABLE AT

WWW.LIFETIMEOFTREASURES.COM
INFO@LIFETIMEOFTREASURES.COM

A HEARTFELT THANK YOU TO OUR READERS

We thank our readers for supporting us in our poetic endeavors. We hope you have been enlightened and uplifted by our life-inspired thoughts of expressions and love. If you have experienced but one emotion, our purpose has been fulfilled.

Notes

WRITTEN THOUGHTS

WRITTEN THOUGHTS